THE
KOALA

A NATION'S ICON

Principal Photographer: Steve Parish

Text: Karin Cox

Steve Parish™

PUBLISHING

THE KOALA

A NATION'S ICON

contents

LEFT: This furred eucalypt dweller with the teddy-bear-like appearance captures the affections of tourists and locals alike.

introduction

Fluffy, notoriously sleepy Koalas occupy a special place in our hearts. They are the slow and steady survivors of the Australian bush — more than any other Australian animal Koalas appear to personify the relaxed, "no worries mate" attitude that is part of the Australian psyche. Despite this harsh, unforgiving continent, these slow-moving marsupials have prospered, colonising the treetops where little appears to disturb their slumber.

I have photographed countless Koalas over the years and the apparent human quality of these personable, charismatic mammals has earned them a "cover model" reputation here at Steve Parish Publishing. The Koala has graced more of my book covers than any other Australian species. Few can resist its cheeky, cuddly charm. There is something in its furry little face, silky ears, curious eyes and bear-like nose that touches the human spirit — reminding us how precious it is to be simply at peace. At the same time, we see in the Koala's struggle to survive that peace is momentary — always there are obstacles, both human and natural, to overcome.

Steve Parish

LEFT: Less commonly seen than kangaroos, these shy treetop dwellers nevertheless keep human admirers captivated by their cuteness.

the
furry face of
Australia

A laid-back personality, well-documented nurturing behaviour and readily recognisable expressions bestow the Koala with a well-deserved cuddly reputation to match its gentle countenance. Aussie kids have grown up with this fluffy icon, some tucked in at night with tales of Blinky Bill, an unlikely hero of the Australian bush; others may clutch a sheepskin "teddy" with a Koala "bear" likeness. It is easy to see why this lovable marsupial originally developed the erroneous name of bear — the Koala's genus name, *Phascolarctos,* means "pouched bear" — but a marsupial it is, its chubby, cute little face suggesting the softer side of a harsh continent. It was not always so, but today the furry-faced Koala is our weak spot — we celebrate the Koala because it appeals to the child in all of us. Somehow this sleepy-headed, vulnerable tree-hugger inspires in us a greater respect for nature.

LEFT: Small children dote on Koalas, perhaps equating them with big, living, breathing, furry soft toys.

Indigenous
tales and
totems

The Koala remains a totemic animal for many Aboriginal people and features in numerous myths and legends. Historical evidence suggests that the Koala was a reliable, easy-to-catch food source, but curiously it seems Aborigines were reluctant to utilise the creatures' dense fur, believing this would have dire consequences. South-eastern Koori people believed watercourses would run dry if a Koala was skinned. A popular Indigenous story is "How the Koala Lost its Tail"; another credits the Koala with invisible powers and a third recounts that the first Aboriginal people to arrive on the continent's east coast did so by travelling over a bridge made from the Koala's incredibly long intestines, which later floated off into the sky and became the first rainbow.

LEFT: Legend has it that the word "Koala" comes from an Aboriginal word from eastern New South Wales, which means "no drink". The names *cullewine, colah, koolah, kaola, koolewong, colo* and *koala* are all Aboriginal dialectical variations recorded in literature since the first European description of a Koala in 1810.

a grim
history

Indigenous Australians did not value Koala fur, but European settlers certainly did. Settlement ushered in a grim period in the Koala's history and millions of Koalas were poached or trapped for their fur. By the late 19th century, the fur market in Europe was receiving up to 300,000 Koala pelts each year. The last Koala "open season" was in August 1927, when 584,738 Koalas were killed in one month. Thankfully, the Koala is now fully protected in Australia.

OPPOSITE AND ABOVE: Koala populations suffered a severe decline during the early 20th century. Despite the 1906 *Native Animals Protection Act*, Koala open seasons continued until Koalas finally became completely protected in the 1930s.

Koala
characters

In 1811, George Perry's illustrated *Arcana; or the Museum of Natural History* states the Koala "is particularly awkward and unwieldy …" and "… we are at a loss to imagine for what particular scale of usefullness [sic] or happiness such an animal could … possibly be destined …" By 1933, however, New Zealand artist Dorothy Wall was so inspired by the "awkward" Koala that she created Blinky Bill, one of the most endearing children's characters of all time. Numerous adventures later, this "Quaint Little Australian" was used as a World War II troop mascot and made it to the big screen in 1992. Inspirationally, KOALA is now the acronym adopted for the "Kids Own Australian Literature Awards".

ABOVE AND OPPOSITE: Dorothy Wall's Blinky Bill and Norman Lindsay's Koala characters are much-loved inventions of Australian art and literature.

living
with
Koalas

Many of the Koala's preferred habitats must be shared with often inconsiderate, sometimes ruthless, competitors — humans. "Koala corridors" along the densely populated east coast try to establish a balance between the needs of Koalas and those of humans, allowing the two mammals to co-exist. Koalas sometimes present themselves in gum trees in backyards or surrounding public parks, much to the delight of humans who discover them, but usually prefer the anonymity of bushland or national parks.

OPPOSITE: Koalas are famously difficult to spot in the treetops, blending in well to their eucalypt domain. ABOVE: If undisturbed, a Koala and joey may visit tall suburban gum trees for a few days.

Koala
parks

Given the scarcity of Koala sightings in the wild, many fauna parks provide the public with an opportunity for direct contact with Koalas. Some are even contributing towards the conservation of Koala habitat. Sick, injured or abandoned animals are the grateful recipients of care and conservation efforts, while the public can gain, first hand, an appreciation of just how vulnerable these cuddly characters are.

OPPOSITE: In the wild, Koalas rarely interact with humans voluntarily. Koala parks and sanctuaries educate Australians and tourists, while simultaneously caring for wildlife.
ABOVE: Adorable Koalas leave a long-lasting impression on young minds.

home among the gum trees

That the Koala exists at all is a miracle of evolution and adaptation, especially considering its fussy feeding habits. Koalas thrive on the leaves and shoots of a limited number of eucalypt trees, making their homes high in tall woodland timbers where they are protected from their less-cumbersome predators. Sclerophyll forest and woodland found down Australia's east coast — from Queensland to New South Wales and westward into Victoria, along with small pockets containing reintroduced Koalas in south-eastern South Australia — is prime Koala habitat. In the treetops, a sturdy trunk to grip onto, succulent leaves to chew, foliage to help obscure and nearby trees to leap into, are the "must-have" features of a fine arboreal abode. Here, Koalas are well-camouflaged, napping up to twenty hours a day in order to conserve the limited energy they glean from a low-nutrient eucalyptus-flavoured diet. Koalas move from their home range reluctantly, only when necessity forces them to search for further food or better shelter, or when fire or drought drive them from their leafy canopies.

LEFT: Several eucalypt species are recognised as the Koala's favourite foods and make the most comfortable dwelling places for these weary marsupials.

Brisbane
&
beyond

A pale grey coat colour and smaller size distinguish the northern subspecies *Phascolarctos cinereus adustus* from its southern relatives. Koalas are widely distributed throughout Queensland but populations are small and are considered regionally vulnerable in parts of South-East Queensland. The Koala Coast region, comprising some suburbs of Brisbane and Logan City, as well as nearby Redland Shire, contains approximately one-fifth of the State's Koala population.

ABOVE, LEFT TO RIGHT: Eucalypt woodlands of the Scenic Rim near the Queensland–New South Wales border. Koala corridors here, and around Brisbane city, coupled with ongoing conservation programs by the Environmental Protection Agency and other wildlife groups, aim to stabilise vulnerable populations in the State's south.

ABOVE, LEFT TO RIGHT: A mother and her tubby joey rest in a well-stocked eucalypt larder; Diet is a major criteria when it comes to habitat selection and most Koalas favour a few food trees in a select area. If necessary, Koalas will also consume *Melaleuca*, *Anghophora* and *Leptospermum* species, although most Queensland Koalas seek out Red Gums, Grey Gums, Swamp Mahogany and Tallowwood.

Sydney &
beyond

Abundant wild places around Sydney should provide sanctuary for Koalas, yet these elusive mammals appear to have vanished in 50–70% of their former range across New South Wales. Such a dramatic decline in Koala numbers has seen them declared vulnerable across the State and recovery plans have been put into action. Where once these placid marsupials enjoyed the hazy, eucalypt-rich Blue Mountains on the city's doorstep, fires have severely impacted on their numbers in the lower Blue Mountains region. Koalas have not been seen in Royal National Park to the city's north since the 1940s.

LEFT: Swathes of eucalypt bushland in Blue Mountains National Park.
ABOVE: This joey will soon leave to establish its own home territory.

Melbourne
& beyond

Koala populations reach their zenith in Victoria. Cooler climate and, in parts, denser tree cover are no obstacle to these hirsute, agile climbers, which are distributed throughout much of the State. Koalas thrive on Phillip Island, French Island, Raymond Island and Quail Island. More than 23,000 Koalas from crowded home ranges have been relocated to over 200 suitable forest homes elsewhere — the largest wildlife reintroduction program on the continent!

LEFT: Victorian Koala habitat. ABOVE: Koalas in Victoria's chilly southern climate have denser fur and are darker in colour than those from the north.

riverine
habitats

An enviable efficiency in processing their food means that Koalas rarely have occasion to drink, thus allowing them to stay safe in the trees where gum leaves provide them with nourishment both solid and liquid. Moisture content in eucalypt leaves is greatest in trees that line watercourses, so stately River Red Gums with "water views" are highly sought after. In drier, inland parts of the Koala's range, most animals are found inhabiting woodland that skirts a network of meandering watercourses.

LEFT: Balancing on an overhanging branch is no impediment to this snoozing riverine inhabitant. ABOVE: Gum leaves provide much of the Koala's water intake.

Koalas
being Koalas

Surprisingly, for animals that appear so affectionate and cuddly, Koalas are not highly sociable. A mosiac of overlapping home ranges brings individuals into relatively frequent contact with their kin, but they remain largely solitary, with each female and joey occupying a few favourite home trees and males dominating a territory that takes in as many females as he can capably satisfy. Koala behaviour seems governed by a strict code of ethics — engage in as little activity as possible! This desire to err on the side of leisure is not due to inherent laziness (or eucalypt intoxication as some early reports of Koala behaviour implied). Rather than live to sleep, Koalas must sleep to live — lots of rest is necessary because the Koala's diet provides little energy to fuel its metabolism. The four or so hours a day that Koalas are active, mostly by moonlight, are taken up with the daily tasks of being a Koala: grooming, feeding, romancing, mating, caring for young, fighting, climbing, and leaping from tree to tree in search of leaves that must meet exacting energy requirements.

LEFT: Koalas are nocturnal, but their night lives are limited to a few hours of arboreal activity before they again take to the boughs and branches that act as Koala bedrooms.

by night & by day

Like most marsupials, Koalas feel safer under the cover of darkness and most of their terrestrial travels are made by night, if at all. Subtle coat colours and the dappled shadows of leaves and branches help the Koala hide in scattered stands of eucalypts by day. When they wedge themselves in the forks of trees, Koalas' hard, padded and densely furred bottoms provide a cushioning layer between themselves and the hard wooden perch.

OPPOSITE: Koalas rarely venture down to the ground, but during breeding season males may set forth in moonlight if the coast is clear. ABOVE: What better way to spend the day than propped on a limb, serene in oblivious slumber?

ABOVE: Few scenes are as adorable as a young Koala snuggled sleepily on a branch or tree trunk.

facial *expression*

A Koala's facial features are similarly proportioned to our own, enabling its face to appear as animated as a human's in expression. Each animal is unique in appearance and personality, and each is capable of expressing nuances of mood. Some appear to smile, grimace or show disinterest. Others appear benignly poised. It is easy for us to equate these expressions with human emotions, but who knows what is going on inside a Koala's head?

ABOVE: A range of expressions — how might you interpret them?

temperature control

In colder habitats, energy, in the form of heat, must be conserved. To stay warm, the Koala tucks its limbs into a tight ball to trap warmth in its thick, waterproof cloak. On hot days, the Koala's dense fur can be a liability. Exposing as much of its body as possible to the breeze, by dangling limbs and draping itself over branches, is the Koala's main strategy for staying cool.

OPPOSITE: When hot, a Koala keeps cool by capturing the breeze on trailing limbs.
ABOVE: When cold, a shaggier pelt, shivering, and curling up into a snug ball helps Koalas keep warm.

treetop
acrobats

Two opposable thumbs and a long, powerful thigh muscle on each hind leg perfectly equip the Koala for a life spent leaping and clambering from tree to tree in the forest canopy. Although hardly graceful, Koalas are highly agile and leaps of two metres between trees have been observed. Sharp claws on the front and back feet tear deep into bark and wood to provide grip (even on slippery surfaces) and often leave behind telltale traces of a Koala's presence.

OPPOSITE AND ABOVE: Epic leaps allow the Koala to move from one home tree to another, but to cover large distances they must risk going down to the ground.

ABOVE, LEFT TO RIGHT: Climbing provides little challenge for these marsupials. The Koala's sturdy physique and padded, rough-soled paws make swinging from branches, balancing on boughs and creeping along limbs easy.

awkward and
ambling
over land

Treetop gymnasts they may be, but at ground level Koalas are at their most cumbersome and susceptible to attack. When on the ground they adopt a comical, ambling quadrupedal gait — unless threatened, when they break into a bounding gallop, heading frantically for the safety of the nearest tree.

BELOW: Startled and exposed, a Koala bounds and runs across an open paddock — much to the bemusement of onlooking cows. RIGHT: The Koala's favoured pace is unhurried — whether on land or in the trees.

OPPOSITE AND RIGHT: For a mother with a young joey on her back, going down to the ground is a great risk. She must remain constantly alert for lurking predators such as Dingoes, dogs and Wedge-tailed Eagles and try to protect her exposed joey.

gum tree
gastronomes

A clever adaptation of the genus *Eucalyptus* was to develop highly toxic leaves in a bid to deter folivores; Koalas have easily thwarted this obstacle. The Koala's nose is finely tuned to sniff out only those leaves for which it has a chemical tolerance. Gum leaves, which are fibrous and woody, are finely chopped up in the mouth before passing to the stomach. The liver filters out toxins and the mass is then passed into a two-metre-long caecum, similar to the human appendix, where bacterial fermentation converts this fibrous pulp into readily digestible nutrients. Not surprisingly, the finicky task of choosing and digesting leaves takes up much of a Koala's few waking hours.

LEFT: Leaf selection is a serious business. Leaves are carefully sniffed to ensure that the species of eucalypt is acceptable.

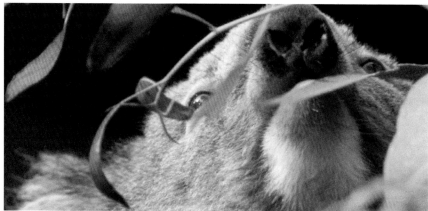

ABOVE: Koalas are famously fussy eaters. Only around eleven of Australia's 700-odd eucalypt species have been identified as Koalas' true preferred food trees. LEFT: Grey Gums support a healthy population of Koalas at Daisy Hill Koala Park in Brisbane. OPPOSITE: Scribbly Gums at Cooloola National Park, Queensland. Scribbly Gum leaves are a staple of a Koala's diet.

grooming
& coat
maintenance

With so much sleep in the Koala's daily itinerary, little time is left for grooming. Thick, fluffy fur, however, can get itchy from time to time as burrs, twigs and sticky gum sap adhere to the dense cloak. Two fused claws on the Koala's hind foot act as a specialised grooming claw, raking through the matted coat and grasping at any small offences to the animal's hygiene and cleanliness.

OPPOSITE AND LEFT: For such rotund creatures, Koalas are remarkably supple. They are able to use their back feet to adeptly scratch an itchy ear, neck or under arm.

Coat colour varies through a range of hues from brown to silvery grey with most differences in colour and shagginess corresponding to a change in climate. In southern areas, Koalas are darker and have denser fur than northern specimens. As a result, three subspecies have been described: *Phascolarctos cinereus cinereus* (NSW), *P. cinereus adustus* (Qld) and *P. cinereus victor* (Vic).

ABOVE, LEFT TO RIGHT: Victorian Koalas are the darkest, fluffiest and heaviest individuals. In the north of their range, Koalas are lighter coloured, less furry and considerably smaller.

Koala
social life

Apart from during breeding season or when forced to partake in territorial battles, most Koalas live largely solitary lives. However, complex rules for interaction in certain "communal" areas still create loosely knit Koala societies high among the gum trees. Home ranges may overlap and trees in these areas are free for all to inhabit, but home food trees — the preferred trees of each individual within a non-overlapping area of its range — are closely guarded. Much discontent arises if an intruder attempts to scale a favoured tree within another Koala's territory. Each home range is carefully surveyed and marked out using scent and scratching, so all members of the society can tell who owns which patch of turf. In the shared trees, Koalas share food, court a suitable partner and mate. So respectful are the Koalas of another's territory that should a member of their community pass to that "great gum tree in the heavens", no-one will move into the vacant territory for almost a year, when the former owner's scent has faded from detection.

LEFT: Fringing stable Koala societies are the young "misfits" who are yet to establish a home range. Juvenile Koalas independent of their mothers may have to wander some distance to find an empty range of their own, take up residence in a "deceased estate" or, if they are males, fight for a chance at dominance.

the
cycle of life

Koalas are both slow-moving and relatively slow-growing with a life cycle that can last up to twenty years in the wild. During this time, Koalas will be born as a tiny, hairless pink "jellybean" that weighs about a gram, take their first tentative steps out of the pouch, learn the secrets of gum leaf selection, assert themselves to acquire a home of their own, find a suitable mate and, if female, go on to give birth to one joey a year — tenderly caring for it until the time comes for the young Koala to make its own way in the world. Mothers are demonstrative with joeys, bestowing maternal affection on them for up to two years. Males, over their lifespan, will fight many times and bear the scars of battle to prove it. One of the most stressful times in a Koala's life is when a home range is compromised by habitat destruction. Strict rules of territory often do not permit a Koala to simply move "next door", forcing it to travel longer distances on a dangerous overland house hunt, should its habitat have been destroyed.

LEFT: The halcyon days of riding piggyback aboard mum last only a short time in the lifespan of a Koala. During this time, the young joey learns the skills it will need to survive on its own.

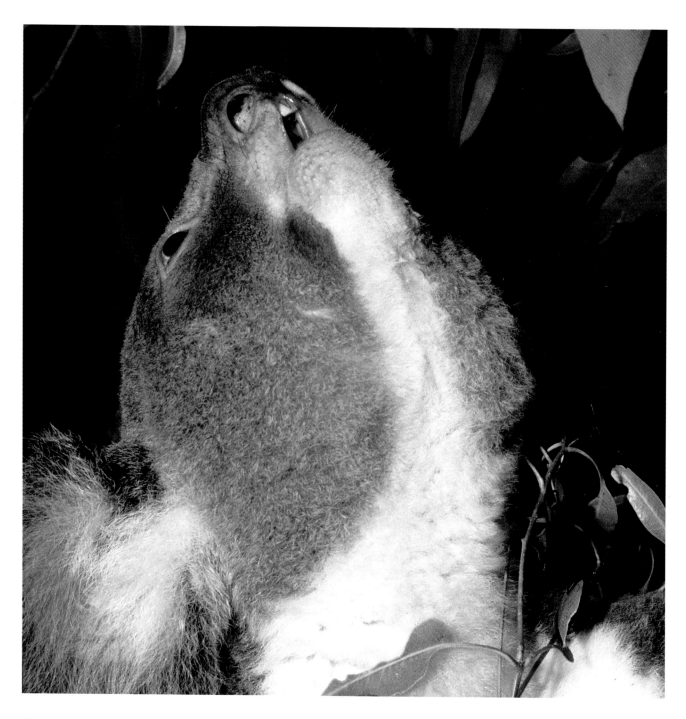

males on the make

From approximately August to February, once-peaceful Koala territory resounds with the roars and bellows of males anxious to find a partner. Mature males, known as bucks, emit loud grunts and snores as a way of letting females and other males know that they are on the make and hunting for a mate.

OPPOSITE: Males are highly vocal during the breeding season. One classic mating behaviour is to point the nose heavenwards and inhale deeply, making a wavering snoring sound. ABOVE: Belching, bellowing and snoring — the Koala's language of courtship.

the scent  of success

Males also secrete a pungent oil from the sternal gland on the chest and use it to smear trees within their territory — leaving a kind of smelly sexual calling card. Females in oestrus respond to this kind of masculine advertising by sending out signals of their own, both wailing and bellowing, and sometimes mimic male behaviour by rubbing their chests up against tree trunks.

OPPOSITE AND ABOVE: Rubbing the chest up and down against tree trunks coats the bark with a sticky, odorous oil and alerts females (by the scent) that a dominant male is on the prowl. Sometimes, home range trees in a female's territory are marked with the urine of the female in oestrus, indicating to the male that a receptive female is nearby.

making a
match

Female Koalas are marsupial feminists and conduct many of the obvious courtship rituals. Passion and aggression seem to be almost one and the same to a frustrated female Koala in oestrus. First, the two paramours will meet in one of her home trees, should she allow it, or in the overlap of their range. To display her readiness, the female may stand up on a tree limb, vigorously jerking her body back and forwards about once a second. Sometimes, especially in captivity, she attempts to inflame her paramour's passion by suggestively mounting another female, or thrusting the male away — only to chase after him, throw her arms around him and bite him coquettishly on the neck. Males are encouraged by this kind of behaviour and so the relationship will be consummated soon afterwards.

OPPOSITE: Courtship, Koala-style. BELOW: Usually solitary creatures, Koalas use loud calls and strong scents to attract mates.

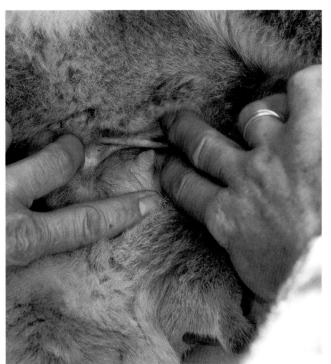
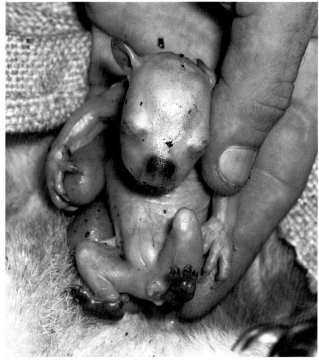

from
pregnancy
to pouch

Approximately 35 days after the Koalas have mated, the female will give birth — a process made somewhat easier than placental mammal births by the fact that the infant is only two centimetres long and weighs about a gram. This miniature, hairless mite clambers into its mother's rear-opening pouch, where it will spend the next five to seven months nestled in. Safe in the pouch, it seizes one of the mother's two teats in its mouth and begins the steady suckling that will see it eventually take on the furry appearance of a Koala.

OPPOSITE: Emerging to a brighter, wilder world. ABOVE, LEFT TO RIGHT: A female Koala has two nipples in her rear-facing pouch to nourish young; A tiny, vulnerable newborn.

a peephole to the world

Elastic and warm, the pouch will be the joey's primary residence until it is fully furred and can venture out. During this time, a tiny inquisitive face may at times peer out, no doubt trying to make sense of the dizzying treetop world. When the fluffy bundle does come out, it will be only temporary at first. During this transitional phase of slowly "weaning" the joey out of the pouch, the little Koala must receive vital gut bacteria that will enable it to digest gum leaves later. A thick green-coloured faecal mix, called pap, is excreted by the mother and consumed by the joey before it moves out of the pouch entirely.

OPPOSITE AND ABOVE: The joey pokes its head out and begins to emerge temporarily and with much trepidation at first.

schooling begins

Once outside the pouch, the lessons of life await. This is a dangerous time in the life of a young joey and its wise mother cuddles it close — the joey clinging to her belly, both for warmth and protection. During this time she will subtly teach her young how an adult Koala conducts its life in the treetops.

OPPOSITE: When a joey reaches around 30 weeks of age, the warmth of the pouch is replaced by the warm embrace of the maternal Koala. Later, the young joey will cling to her back. ABOVE: A proud mother and her joey.

taking a back seat

By 36 weeks of age, the chubby joey is getting far too big to attempt to re-enter the pouch or be cuddled on its mother's tummy. Another change occurs — the equivalent of moving from baby seat to back passenger seat — and joey now rides up high on its mother's sturdy back. A tight grip is vital. If the joey falls off and plummets to the ground, the mistake could be fatal — its mother may not always retrieve it. In captivity, Koala mothers appear to be quite content with any infant on their back, whether it is their joey or not.

OPPOSITE AND ABOVE: Joeys riding on a mother's back have a high vantage point — perfect for selecting fresh young leaves and keeping watch for predators.

RIGHT: In crowded areas where there are many overlapping territories, a joey's independence may be somewhat stifled. It such areas young Koalas often stay with their mothers for longer and may grow quite heavy before they give up their parental perch and set off on their own.

ABOVE, LEFT TO RIGHT: Young Koalas are shy and very reluctant to leave mother's back; At first, even when they do so, they make sure that mum is still within arm's reach, not daring to venture more than a metre away from her reassuring side; In inclement weather, or when afraid, joeys may even creep around to seek the shelter of her maternal embrace.

LEFT AND ABOVE: Until the joey grows teeth, at around 24 weeks of age, eating tough, fibrous gum leaves is out of the question. By the time it takes up its piggybacking position, a joey's diet consists of gum leaves and its mother's milk.

starting
to stray

There comes a time in every mammal's life when independence beckons. For a young Koala, the move to independence is a hesitant one. From about 37 weeks of age the young Koala moves tentatively away from its mother in the treetops, but quickly cancels its sojourn and squeaks with alarm if its mother begins to move away, or if it becomes afraid. Even at 44 weeks, the joey stays within leaping distance of its protector; although, within a month it grows more courageous, gradually venturing further from her side.

RIGHT: Joeys prefer to stay close to their mothers until they reach about 48 weeks of age. At this time, mothers and joeys are sometimes seen back-to-back, enjoying the other's closeness and warmth.

getting the
hang
of it

THESE PAGES: Most juvenile mammals are playful and gregarious, but due to the Koala's largely solitary lifestyle and low energy levels, joeys rarely play for the sake of play alone. Climbing is probably the only real Koala "play", with juveniles mastering the slippery secret of their arboreal existence — clambering over, swinging under, hanging from — and pulling themselves up onto tree branches.

ABOVE AND OPPOSITE: With its finely tuned sense of smell a young Koala investigates a branch, possibly searching out the resinous aromas of its favourite leafy meal or the scent markings of other animals.

staking a claim

Little more than a year into their young lives, juvenile Koalas must set up home for themselves. Finding suitable arboreal accommodation is more difficult in regions where Koala numbers are high, or where habitat borders areas of human habitation. Sometimes, a young Koala can take up residency in a vacant range if the former occupant has died; others loiter on the fringes of Koala society, using communal trees and being perpetually moved along until they can find a stretch of habitat to call their own. In lean times, or in tightly packed territories, a female may remain in its mother's range for up to three years.

OPPOSITE AND ABOVE: **A home range is staked out by scratching and scenting.**

LEFT AND ABOVE: A Koala's territory usually constitutes only a few hectares. This small parcel of land must provide plenty of shelter and enough food trees for the Koala to sustain itself. In the case of females, such territory must also support future offspring.

Koala elders

Notwithstanding the Koala's vulnerability, these marsupials exhibit a longevity that may see them survive up to 20 years, although most have a lifespan of 6–15 years. Males, due to the hierarchical nature of Koala society and the perils of fighting, have a maximum lifespan of around 13 years. Even in their dotage, elderly male Koalas will have to cantankerously assert their dominance over young males in order to keep their homes in retirement.

THESE PAGES: An elderly Koala is hard to identify, but perhaps looks even wearier than most.

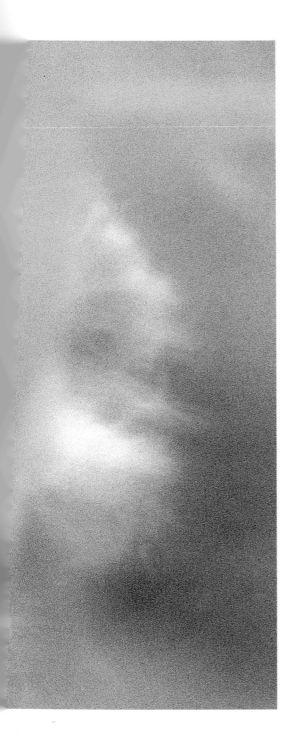

survival
— a Koala's
perspective

How such a specialised, leisurely, slow-breeding and sluggish creature evolved is one thing; how it continues to survive in a rapidly paced world is another. Koalas face threats both natural and artificial — of these, humankind is perhaps the most dangerous. Thankfully, since the heady, greedy days of settlement, many humans have recognised just how much Koalas require our protection. Predators, both in the sky and on land, consider the lethargic Koala an easy meal. Dogs, Dingoes and large feral cats are far superior ground combatants, while in the treetops, pythons and Wedge-tailed Eagles frequently abscond with juveniles. Roads and fences bisect Koala territory, making moving for mating or social purposes a dangerous, frequently deadly, exercise. With a single lightning strike or careless flick of a match, fire can decimate entire populations. These factors, combined with the Koala's slow reproductive rate and high rate of chlamydia (a sexually transmitted disease causing infertility, blindness and pneumonia), seriously threaten the Koala's long-term continued existence.

LEFT: Tall trees and a luxuriant coverage of gum leaves offer Koalas some measure of protection, but Koalas are no match for predators or humans.

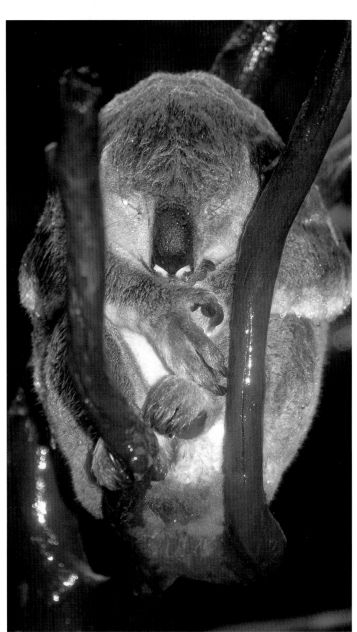

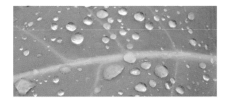

weathering
storms

Of all marsupials, Koalas have the thickest, most insulating fur. Natural oils from the skin give it waterproof qualities, while the fur is denser on the back, making the Koala's "raincoat" even more effective when its arms are tucked protectively over the thinner, fluffier hair on its stomach.

THESE PAGES: Wedging its body tight in a tree fork, curled into a ball, is the Koala's strategy for surviving a tempest.

surviving
floods

The Koala's preference for altitude mostly serves it well during floods, however severe flooding can fell trees and unlucky Koalas who fall into the floodwaters have to swim to safety, seeking a stand of eucalypts in which to shelter until the waters subside. Koalas are not strong swimmers and swim using a kind of awkward "Koala paddle", frantically drawing each forearm under the body.

ABOVE: Swimming is usually reserved for circumstances where Koalas must breach small streams, creeks or rivers. Long-distance swimming does not suit the Koala's stout physique. RIGHT: Eucalypts with interlocking canopies provide refuge.

TODAY'S FIRE DANGER

fleeing

Of all natural disasters, fire is the most destructive to Koalas. Faster, fitter marsupials might be able to flee on foot, but the Koala's arboreal physique denies it this strategy. A keen sense of smell helps it detect smoke from quite a distance, but its best defence is to leap from tree to tree until it reaches a watercourse, where fire is largely thwarted. Tall eucalypts may weather the inferno, but even so, survivors face burns, starvation and infection.

THESE PAGES: Koalas must flee fire, the natural scourge of the Australian bush. Following bushfire many scorched and singed survivors are rescued and relocated to wildlife sanctuaries.

airborne enemies

One disadvantage of having your young perched enticingly on your back is attack by airborne predators. Plucking a joey off its frightened mother's back is a simple task for a large Wedge-tailed Eagle and many Koalas meet their fate in the rapacious beak of this "shark of the skies". Larger owls and other raptor species will also attempt to snatch and devour joeys if given the opportunity.

OPPOSITE: Mothers need to keep an alert eye on the skies.
ABOVE, LEFT AND RIGHT: Some birds are fearsome predators swooping down to carry off joeys, if they can grab them, whether in the branches or on the ground.

destruction of habitat

Intricate laws of range ownership and social interaction, coupled with the Koala's dietary reliance on specific eucalypt species, exacerbate the dangers of habitat destruction. If the vital food or home trees are cleared, Koalas are forced to move, but cannot simply move next door into the territory of another. Thus, wanton habitat destruction is one of the largest Koala killers.

ABOVE AND OPPOSITE: Unfortunately, a preferential habitat for Koalas is often woodlands near the coast, where humans also like to live. As much as 80% of the Koala's former distribution range has been cleared for agriculture or development.

the road to ruin

Habitat destruction, fences, and power poles aside, humans are also responsible for creating another mass murderer of our iconic Koalas — roads and freeways. Koalas are ill-equipped to move rapidly on the ground, let alone avoid cars when blinded by headlights and frozen in fear. Unfortunately, the death of a mother is usually fatal for pouch young or joeys travelling on her back.

OPPOSITE, LEFT AND RIGHT: In the wild, Koalas are often noticed only when they reach the roadside and are sometimes seen only too late. LEFT: Signs warn motorists to take care at likely "Koala crossings". ABOVE: Making a dash for it.

dogs
— a savage
threat

For Koalas, dogs represent danger on four legs. That gentle, ambling Koalas could provide sport for a pack of well-fed suburban canines is one of Nature's little cruelties. Caught on the ground, Koalas have little chance of defending themselves or their young. Domestic dogs and cars are two of the Koala biggest threats. Combined, these two threats kill more than 4000 Koalas a year. Dingoes are also fierce predators of Koalas on the ground.

OPPOSITE AND ABOVE: Caution is entirely necessary for Koalas around farms and suburbs, where dangers lurk; suburban fear and panic for a mother and joey.

the Koala's
only kin:
the wombat

Only one other living creature can claim kinship with the Koala, and although still only a distant relation, the physiological similarities are enough to place both animals in the suborder Vombatiformes. Rotund, burrowing wombats are perhaps a little further up the mental evolutionary chain. The wombat has a large brain relative to its overall body mass (thought to indicate a high level of intelligence), but physically they almost appear to be "ground Koalas". Like Koalas, the wombat has a short, stumpy tail; raises its young in a rear-facing pouch; has a diet that is high in fibre and low in nutrients, and is covered in a thick, furry coat. Unlike Koalas, wombats spend their entire lives on the ground. Wombat teeth are very different to those of the Koala, to match the differences in their diets. Wombats mainly eat grass, which they shear from the ground with rootless, rodent-like incisors (which continue to grow throughout their lives). Both Koalas and wombats have a home territory, but the wombat's is larger, ranging from 5–23 hectares.

LEFT: The wombat is the Koala's closest living relative. Many more Koala-like ancestors, closer in form than the wombat, existed in prehistoric times.

body
&
build

THESE PAGES: When put through its paces the naturally arboreal Koala is no match for the terrestrial Wombat.

From a distance, a Koala on the ground could almost be mistaken for a wombat. Up close, there are obvious differences. Wombats move with a quadrupedal gait, but are not as ungainly as Koalas and can move much faster. At pace, a wombat can move at speeds of up to 40 kilometres an hour — much faster than the half-bounding/half-running Koala.

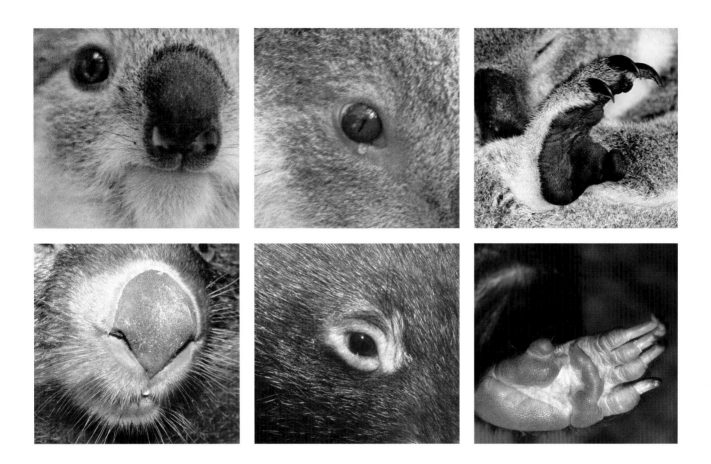

features & senses

Superficial similarities between Koalas and wombats are undermined by differences. The Koala's nose is oblong and its nostrils more rounded than that of the wombat. Koalas' eyes are more forward facing than wombats', allowing them to accurately gauge distance. Wombats' muscular forelimbs are well-suited to excavation, while the Koala's similar muscle structure helps it to climb. The thumb on the Koala's hind foot is well developed to suit its arboreal life, whereas the wombat's foot structure is better suited to life on the ground.

OPPOSITE: A brown Common Wombat foraging through vegetation. ABOVE, TOP TO BOTTOM: Koala and wombat: Physical features reflect their different lifestyles.

different
lifestyles

Nocturnal activity suits both the wombat and the Koala, and both survive on a herbivorous diet, but that is one of the few commonalities in their lifestyles. Wombats live almost two-thirds of their lives underground, conserving energy in cool caverns, which they spend much time digging and renovating; they cannot climb, just as the Koala is not designed for burrowing. The word that aptly springs to mind when thinking of wombats is "waddle". They certainly aren't capable of the nimble balancing acts that Koalas undertake daily.

OPPOSITE: Wombats carefully dig out a burrow that is approximately 50 centimetres wide by 50 centimetres high. ABOVE: Cautious Koalas seek the protection of the trees.

caring
for
young

Wombat mothers are nurturing and affectionate, but few mothers share the tender reputation of the sweet Koala mum. Like all marsupial babies, infant wombats are known as joeys and are born blind, hairless and underdeveloped. Their migration from pouch to paws happens much faster than that of a baby Koala. Once a wombat joey leaves the pouch it is unable to hitch a lift; instead it stays by its mother's side for five to ten months before leaving to seek a home range of its own.

OPPOSITE: Baby wombats are independent by about ten months of age. ABOVE: Koalas require — and receive — mother's protection for a year, sometimes more.

the Common Wombat

Obviously the most widely distributed of the three wombat species, the Common Wombat burrows in eucalypt forest, woodland and coastal heath throughout much of New South Wales' east coast, Tasmania and south-eastern Victoria. Thick fur ranging in shade from a brownish black to a cream colour keeps them warm in the temperate southern climate. Common Wombats are able to breed all year round, although, like Koalas, they only give birth to one infant per year. Common Wombats are easily distinguished from the related hairy-nosed species by their naked, furless noses.

OPPOSITE: Open grassy areas are favoured feeding sites. ABOVE: Fur ranges in colour but always blends in well with woodland habitats.

the Northern Hairy-nosed Wombat

Little more than 300 hectares in Queensland's Epping Forest National Park stand between this critically endangered species and extinction. Around 80–100 members of the world's only population of Northern Hairy-nosed Wombats are protected in this haven by a Dingo-proof fence, yet still they face threats from fire and drought. Long silky hair and longer, pointed ears tufted with white are the hallmarks of this wombat, the largest of the wombat species.

OPPOSITE: Conservation efforts to rescue the Northern Hairy-nosed Wombat are underway. ABOVE: Members of this species may share burrows, but usually they feed alone.

the Southern
Hairy-nosed
Wombat

Semi-arid, sandy plains of Australia's southern eucalypt woodlands are home to scattered colonies of Southern Hairy-nosed Wombats. While not as endangered as Northern Hairy-nosed Wombats, Southern Hairy-nosed Wombats occupy a much smaller range than their Common Wombat cousins. They mature more slowly than other wombat species, with females reaching breeding age at three years. During drought, breeding ceases entirely, making them highly susceptible to climate change.

OPPOSITE: White hair sometimes grows on the hairy nose of this species.
ABOVE: The portly Southern Hairy-nosed Wombat can weigh up to 32 kilograms.

151

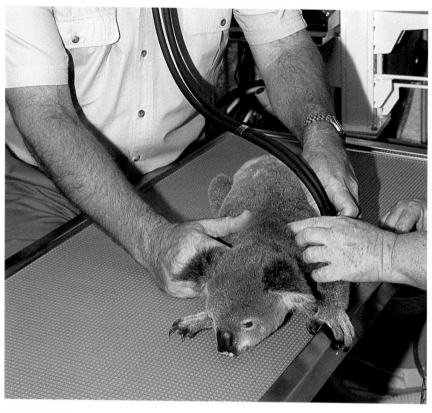

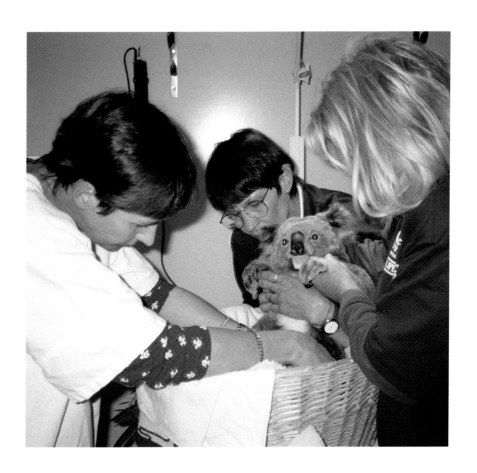

Koala
research, care &
conservation

An obvious fragility about this funny-faced, furry Australian icon inspires people to care about its fate. Wild populations, which have been severely threatened by the disease chlamydia, are monitored by wildlife services around the country. Registered Koala carers take in orphaned or injured joeys. Koalas in captivity, as well as wild individuals, have featured in several research programs — allowing experts to discover more about one of the continent's most engaging and environmentally challenged mammals.

THESE PAGES: Injured Koalas should immediately be taken to a vet surgery, where they may be aided, microchipped and released, or taken to a sanctuary.

fauna
education

Education is an essential aspect of conservation. Most Australians and tourists will never have the privilege of seeing a Koala or wombat in the wild; wombats are a rare sight even for most wildlife watchers. Learning more about these cuddly marsupials, and teaching children about Koalas (in particular, the importance of habitat protection — especially in Australia's eucalypt woodlands), can go some way towards preserving these mammals for future generations.

OPPOSITE: Cuddling a Koala at Lone Pine Koala Sanctuary, Brisbane.
ABOVE: A young boy makes his acquaintance with a Common Wombat at Currumbin Wildlife Sanctuary, Gold Coast.

"What we have to learn to do,
we learn by doing."

Aristotle, Greek Philosopher, Nicomachean Ethics.

I hope this book inspires you not only to cherish our native Australian Koala, but also spurs you into action to ensure its continued survival. Along with Koalas, we too share a common, fragile existence on this planet. Perhaps Koalas remind us of our own fragility, stirring our conscience and human spirit to further protect and conserve our precious natural environment before it is too late.

— STEVE PARISH

Finding Koalas

During the day look up into forked trees for sleeping Koalas. Check smooth tree trunks for pock marks and short, parallel gouges. Look on the ground for walking or bounding tracks with wide-soled, five-digit prints. Look around the base of trees for brown or reddish-brown droppings that are hard, ridged and cylindrical. Green-tinged droppings may be found during the breeding season. Track Koalas at night by their loud bellows, snore-like grunts, wails and screams.

Front foot and print

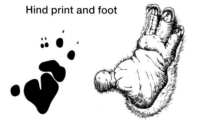
Hind print and foot

KOALA DISTRIBUTION MAP

LOCATION TIPS

- Kangaroo Island, SA
- Grampians NP, Vic
- Brisbane Forest Park, Qld
- Myall Lakes NP, NSW

Finding Wombats

Look along dry watercourses, gullies and on sloping hills above creeks on cloudless evenings. Try overcast winter days in the snow country. A cluster of entrance holes fronted by piles of rubble is the most obvious sign. Wombats have large flat feet and a pigeon-toed gait, and leave distinctive tracks. Look for large cube-shaped droppings on prominent logs and rocks. Wombats often leave hair on smoothly polished rubbing posts, such as tree trunks, logs and stumps.

Front foot and print   Hind print and foot

WOMBAT DISTRIBUTION MAPS

Common Wombat

Southern
Hairy-nosed Wombat

Northern
Hairy-nosed Wombat

LOCATION TIPS

- Kosciuszko NP, NSW
- Wilsons Promontory NP, Vic
- Messent CP, SA
- Cradle Mountain–
  Lake St Clair NP, Tas
- Nullarbor Plain, SA & WA
- Epping Forest NP, Qld

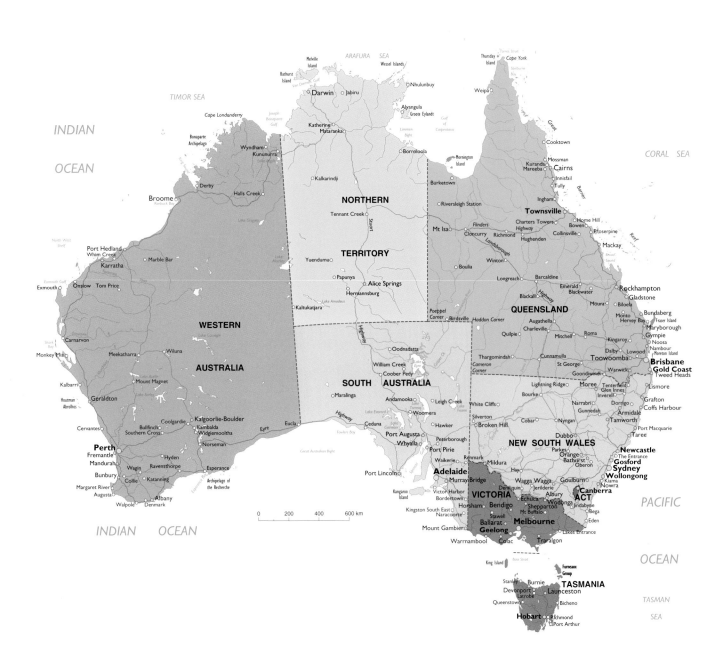

INDIAN
OCEAN

TIMOR SEA

ARAFURA SEA

Cape Londonderry

Melville
Island

Bathurst
Island

Wessel Islands

Thursday
Island

Cape York

CORAL SEA

Bonaparte
Archipelago

Wyndham
Kununurra

Darwin

Jabiru

Nhulunbuy

Alyangula
Groote Eylandt

Weipa

Broome

Derby

Halls Creek

Kalkarindji

Katherine

Mataranka

Borroloola

Gulf
of
Carpentaria

Mornington
Island

Burketown

Cooktown

Kuranda
Mareeba

Mossman

Cairns

Innisfail

Tully

North West
Shelf

Port Hedland
Whim Creek

Karratha

Marble Bar

Riversleigh Station

Mt Isa

Cloncurry

Richmond

Hughenden

Charters Towers
Highway

Collinsville

Ingham

Home Hill

Townsville

Bowen

Proserpine

Mackay

Exmouth
Gulf

Exmouth

Onslow

Tom Price

Papunya

Yuendumu

Alice Springs

Hermannsburg

Boulia

Winton

Longreach

Barcaldine

Emerald
Blackwater

Moura

Rockhampton

Gladstone

Biloela

WESTERN

AUSTRALIA

Carnarvon

Monkey Mia

Meekatharra

Wiluna

Mount Magnet

Kaltukatjara

Poeppel
Corner

Birdsville

Haddon Corner

QUEENSLAND

Blackall

Augathella

Charleville

Mitchell

Roma

Emerald

Monto
Hervey Bay

Fraser Island

Maryborough

Gympie

Noosa

Shark Bay

Kalbarri

Houtman
Abrolhos

Geraldton

SOUTH AUSTRALIA

Maralinga

Oodnadatta

William Creek

Coober Pedy

Cameron
Corner

Thargomindah

Cunnamulla

St George

Toowoomba

Goondiwindi

Warwick

Dalby

Kingaroy

Lowood

Nambour
Moreton I.

Brisbane

Gold Coast
Tweed Heads

Cervantes

Bulfinch
Southern Cross

Coolgardie

Kalgoorlie-Boulder

Kambalda
Widgiemooltha

Norseman

Eucla

Eyre

Highway

Lake Eyre

Andamooka

Leigh Creek

Woomera

White Cliffs

Silverton

Broken Hill

Cobar

Lightning Ridge

Bourke

Moree

Narrabri

Gunnedah

Tenterfield

Glen Innes
Inverell

Dorrigo

Armidale

Tamworth

Lismore

Grafton

Coffs Harbour

Port Macquarie

Taree

Perth

Fremantle
Mandurah

Hyden

Ravensthorpe

Wagin

Esperance

Ceduna

Fowlers Bay

Hawker

Peterborough

Port Augusta

Whyalla

Port Pirie

NEW SOUTH WALES

Dubbo

Nyngan

Parkes

Orange

Bathurst
Oberon

Dubbo

Newcastle

The Entrance

Gosford

Sydney

Wollongong

Kiama
Nowra

Bunbury

Collie

Katanning

Margaret River

Augusta

Walpole

Denmark

Albany

Great Australian Bight

Port Lincoln

Kangaroo
Island

Adelaide

Murray
Bridge

Waikerie

Renmark

Mildura

Hay

Wagga Wagga

Deniliquin

Jerilderie

Albury

Goulburn

Canberra

ACT

Jindabyne

Bega

PACIFIC

Kingston South East

Naracoorte

Bordertown

Horsham

VICTORIA

Echuca

Shepparton

Wodonga

Mt Buffalo

Eden

Stawell

Bendigo

Ballarat

Geelong

Melbourne

Colac

Traralgon

Lakes Entrance

Mount Gambier

Warrnambool

King Island

Bass Strait

Furneaux
Group

OCEAN

TASMAN

SEA

Stanley

Burnie

Queenstown

Devonport
Latrobe

Launceston

Bicheno

TASMANIA

Hobart

Richmond

Port Arthur

INDIAN   OCEAN

0   200   400   600 km

159

Acknowledgements:

A big thank you to Dr Greg Gordon, Damian McGreevy and Dr Steve Brown who first introduced me to these wonderful animals in the wild and in captivity in South-East Queensland.

Thanks to my many associates that work with and care for Koalas in Australia's zoos, national parks, reserves and fauna parks, particularly at Featherdale Wildlife Park (Sydney), Currumbin Sanctuary (Gold Coast), Healesville Sanctuary (Victoria), and Cleland Conservation Park (South Australia).

Each have contributed by permitting me to make close physical contact with Koalas, which has been essential for making many of the images in this book. Finally, I would like to commend the brave efforts of the staff of the Australian Koala Foundation for their tireless work in bringing the plight of the Koala to public attention — my hat goes off to you.

First Published in 2007 by
Steve Parish Publishing Pty Ltd
PO Box 1058, Archerfield, Qld 4108 Australia

© copyright Steve Parish Publishing

Photography: Steve Parish.

Additional photography: Ken Griffiths/ANTPhoto.com: p. 20; Jon Hanger/ANTPhoto.com: pp. 60–1; Ford Kristo/ANTPhoto.com: p. 129 (right); Fredy Mercay/ANTPhoto.com: pp. 42–3, 52, 59, 80, 129 (left), 138 (top) & 142; Fred Parker/ANTPhoto.com: p. 126 (bottom left); Chris & Sandra Pollitt/ANTPhoto.com: pp. 78, 84 & 87; Dave Watts/ANTPhoto.com: pp. 74, 144 & 148–9; Martin Willis/ANTPhoto.com: p. 44; Theo Allofs/Auscape: p. 133 (right); John-Paul Ferrero/Auscape: pp. 16, 89, 132, 138 (bottom) & 152 (bottom left); Oxford Scientific Films/Auscape: p. 122; Emma Harm: p. 68 (left); Greg Harm: p. 133 (left); Collection: John Oxley Library, State Library of Queensland, #18937: p. 13; Gary Bell/OceanwideImages.com: pp. 40 & 134; Mitchell Library, State Library of New South Wales: p. 12; Gary Steer: pp. 58, 102–3, 123 (left), 124, 131 (bottom left & right), 135, 152 (top left) & 153; Clare Thomson: p. 126 (bottom right)

Illustrations: *The Complete Adventures of Blinky Bill,* by Dorothy Wall, published by Angus & Robertson, 1939: p. 14; Norman Lindsay, © H. C. & A. Glad, National Library of Australia, #nla.pic.vn3255433: p. 15

Text: Karin Cox, SPP

Design: Leanne Nobilio, SPP

Editorial: Mary Ann Ghaffurian, Ted Lewis, Michele Perry, SPP; Britt Winter

Production: Wendy Mansell, SPP

First published 2007
ISBN: 978174193283 6

Prepress by Colour Chiefs Digital Imaging, Brisbane, Australia
Printed in China by Everbest Printing Co Ltd.

Produced in Australia at the Steve Parish Publishing Studios

FRONT AND BACK COVERS: Koala and joey.
ABOVE: Koalas where they are most comfortable — in the fork of a gum.